The Soon Life

Phoebe McIntosh

I0141063

methuen | drama

LONDON • NEW YORK • OXFORD • NEW DELHI • SYDNEY

METHUEN DRAMA
Bloomsbury Publishing Plc, 50 Bedford Square, London, WC1B 3DP, UK
Bloomsbury Publishing Inc, 1359 Broadway, New York, NY 10018, USA
Bloomsbury Publishing Ireland, 29 Earlsfort Terrace, Dublin 2,
D02 AY28, Ireland

BLOOMSBURY, METHUEN DRAMA and the Methuen
Drama logo are trademarks of Bloomsbury Publishing Plc.

First published in Great Britain 2025

For legal purposes the Acknowledgements on p. vii
constitute an extension of this copyright page.

Cover Image by Suzi Corker

No rights in incidental music or songs contained in the work are hereby granted
and performance rights for any performance/presentation whatsoever must be
obtained from the respective copyright owners.

All rights whatsoever in this play are strictly reserved and application for
performance etc. should be made before rehearsals begin. No performance
may be given unless a licence has been obtained.

A catalogue record for this book is available from the British Library.

Library of Congress Control Number: 2025946129

ISBN: PB: 978-1-3505-4703-2
ePDF: 978-1-3505-4704-9
eBook: 978-1-3505-4705-6

Series: Modern Plays

Typeset by Mark Heslington Ltd, Scarborough, North Yorkshire

For product safety related questions contact
productsafety@bloomsbury.com.

To find out more about our authors and books visit
www.bloomsbury.com and sign up for our newsletters.

THE SOON LIFE

Cast and Creative Team

Written by	**Phoebe McIntosh**
Directed by	**Sarah Meadows**
Performed by	**Phoebe McIntosh & Joe Boylan**
Set & Costume Design	**Sarah Beaton**
Lighting Design	**Alex Musgrave**
Sound Design & Composition	**Beth Duke**
Movement Direction & Intimacy Coordination	**Tian Brown-Sampson**
Costume & Props Assistant	**Shannon Blackwood**
Videography	**Rich Rusk**
Photography	**Suzi Corker**
Communications Coordinator	**Velenzia Spearpoint**
Press & Publicity	**Chloe Nelkin PR**
Programme & Playtext	**Methuen Drama**
Panel Discussions	**Birthrights & Make Birth Better**
Dramaturgy	**Robert Awosusi**
Doula Consultants	**Nikita Akilapa & Suzie Kamau**
Dance Coach	**Aneta Zwierzynska**
Stage Management	**Jasmin Meara Wall**
Production Management	**Joe Prentice**
Project Management	**Maeve O'Neill**
Produced by	**Rua Arts, Phoebe McIntosh**

Supported by **Talawa Theatre Company, Soho Theatre, Jacksons Lane and Birth Supplies (DPEK Healthcare)**

Funded by **Arts Council England National Lottery, Royal Victoria Hall Foundation and Crowdfunding**

BIOGRAPHIES

Phoebe McIntosh – Writer and performer playing Bec

Phoebe McIntosh (she/her) is an actor, author and playwright based in London. As a performer her works spans stage, screen and audio. She wrote and performed in a sell-out run of her first play, *The Tea Diaries*, at the Edinburgh Fringe Festival in 2013, followed by her solo show, *Dominoes*, which toured the South East and London in 2018. She has been a selected writer on the Soho Theatre Writers' Lab, Tamasha Playwrights and Talawa Firsts and her play, *The Soon Life*, won the highly commended prize at the Tony Craze Awards 2020 as well as being longlisted for the Alfred Fagon Award 2020, the Bruntwood Prize 2022 and the Theatre503 International Playwrighting Award 2023. Phoebe won a place on the inaugural Tamasha x Hachette creative writing programme and was also selected for the Penguin Random House WriteNow programme in 2020. Her novel *Dominoes*, adapted from the solo show, was published by Chatto & Windus (UK) and Penguin Random House (US) before going on to being longlisted for the Bath Novel Award 2021, the Waterstones Debut Fiction Prize 2024, and the Authors' Club Best First Novel Award 2025.

Sarah Meadows – Director

Sarah (she/her) is an award-winning director of plays and musicals. Current projects include: North American tour of her award winning production of the musical *Ride*, which had its critically acclaimed US premier at San Diego's Old Globe Theatre in spring 2024; *Lourdes! A Musical!* by Xnthony/music by Matthew Floyd Jones premiering autumn 2026. In the UK, *Ride* received critical acclaim and was a finalist for six Off West End Awards nominations including Best Director. *Ride* was also a finalist for Best Off-West End Production at the 2022 WhatsOnStage Awards and various other awards including Broadway World. Sarah was a director with the prestigious Old Vic 12, co-artistic director of Longsight Theatre Company and was associate director on the West End and UK tour to Tony award winning Daniel Aukin (*Stereophonic*) for the Broadway transfer of Joshua Harmon's *Admissions* and Sir Richard Eyre on the West End production and tour of *Blithe Spirit* (starring Jennifer Saunders). Recent credits include: *Marie Curie* (Charing Cross Theatre); *The Good Enough Mums Club* (Birmingham Hippodrome/UK tour); *One Jewish Boy* (Trafalgar Studios); *Bricks* (Old Vic). Sarah is represented by Intertalent in the UK and Gersh in the USA.

Instagram: @sarahmeadowsdirector

Joe Boylan – Performer playing Alex

Joe Boylan (he/him) is a very experienced theatre actor and has performed in theatres around the country. He graduated from Lamda MA course in 2022 and is the founding member of the Barrel Organ Theatre Company. Theatre credits include: *The Glorious French Revolution* (New Diorama Theatre); *The Snow Queen* (Polka Theatre); *Accidental Death of an Anarchist* (Royal Theatre Haymarket); *I Want My Hat Back* (Angel Theatre/tour); *The Great Christmas Feast* (The Lost Estate); *Tess* (English Touring Theatre and Barrel Organ); *Some People Talk About Violence* (Royal Exchange Theatre, Manchester); *Me and My Bee* (UK and international tour); *Winkey* (Soho Theatre). Instagram: @joeboylan_

Sarah Beaton – Set & Costume Design

Sarah (she/her) is a performance designer and visual dramaturge. She studied Design for Stage at The Central School of Speech and Drama, graduating in 2011 with first class honours. Later that year she was awarded The Linbury Prize for Stage Design. From 2015 to 2016 she was the designer on attachment at The Old Vic. Her work has been exhibited at the National Theatre, World Stage Design (Cardiff); the V&A and World Stage Design (Taiwan). Theatre work includes: *The Lightest Element, The Harmony Test, Nineteen Gardens, Mother Christmas* (Hampstead Theatre); *Carmen* (Scottish Opera); *The Merchant of Venice* (Shakespeare's Globe); *Babur in London* (Sadler's Wells); *Wild East* (Young Vic); *Mum* (Plymouth Theatre Royal/Soho); *Faust* (Altes Schauspielhaus, Germany); *La Bohème* (Longborough Festival Opera); *The Human Voice* (Gate); *Building the Wall* (Park Theatre); *Crocodiles* (Manchester Royal Exchange); *Spitfire Girls, The School for Scandal, The Picture of Dorian Gray* (national tours); *Possession, Great Apes, The Double Act* (Arcola); *Rise* (Old Vic); *In Event of Moon Disaster* (Theatre503); *One Who Wants to Cross* (Finborough Theatre); *Diary of a Madman* (Sherman Theatre); *Mix the Play* (Old Vic); *Missing, Run, Gap in the Light* (Engineer Theatre Collective).

www.sarahbeaton.com Instagram: @beaton_s

Alex Musgrave – Lighting Design

Alex (he/him) designs lighting for theatre, musicals and opera across the UK and internationally. Upcoming work: *The Forsyte Saga this Christmas at the RSC Stratford*. Recent design work includes: *Home* (Chichester Festival Theatre); *The White Rose* (Marylebone Theatre); *Figaro:*

An Original Musical (London Palladium); *A Christmas Carol* (The Lowry, Manchester); *The Forsyte Saga – Parts 1 & 2* (Park Theatre, Finsbury Park); *Stones in His Pockets* (Barn Theatre, Cirencester, Salisbury Playhouse and Bolton Octagon); *The White Factory, The Last Word* (Marylebone Theatre); *Unbound – a New Musical, A Concert* (Hoxton Hall); *Kin – The Musical* (Teatro Technis, London); *Before After, Romeo and Juliet* (Southwark Playhouse); *It's a MotherF**king Pleasure* (North American tour, SoHo Playhouse – New York City, Southbank Centre and Soho Theatre – London, national and European tours); *Sherlock and the Whitechapel Fiend, Treasure Island* and *Private Lives* (Barn Theatre, Cirencester); *The Cunning Little Vixen* (Royal Birmingham Conservatoire); *Rapunzel* (The Watermill Theatre). Alex was the Association of Lighting Production and Design Lumière 2019 and has been nominated for two Off West End Awards for Best Lighting Design for *The White Factory* at the Marylebone Theatre and *You Are Here* at the Southwark Playhouse. Instagram: @ amusgravelightingdesign

Beth Duke – Sound Design & Composition

Beth (she/her) is a sound designer and composer based in London. She studied Theatre Sound at the Royal Central School of Speech and Drama. Beth's experience covers a wide range of theatre, plays, musicals and events. She was recently nominated for an Offie Award for Best Sound Design, and was resident sound designer at the Almeida Theatre. Credits include: *Retrograde* (Kiln Theatre and Apollo Theatre); *Silence* (Queen's Theatre Hornchurch and UK tour); *Coming to England* (Nicoll Entertainment, UK tour); *Bedroom Farce* (Queens Theatre Hornchurch); *Hasbian* (Clapham Omnibus); *Party Games* (Yvonne Arnold Theatre and tour); *The Other Boleyn Girl* (Chichester Festival Theatre); *Sherlock Holmes and the Poison Wood, The Suspicions of Mr Whicher* (Watermill Theatre); *Richard, My Richard*

(Shakespeare North Playhouse); *The Jolly Christmas Postman* (Royal & Derngate); *The Frogs* (Royal Derngate/Kiln Theatre); *Wishmas: A Fantastical Christmas Adventure* (Secret Group); *Jack and the Beanstalk* (Stratford East); *Syncopation* (Bridewell Theatre); *What It Means* (Wilton's Music Hall); *Strategic Love Play* (Belgrade Theatre/Soho Theatre/UK tour); *The Trial of Josie K* (Unicorn Theatre); *Akedah* (Hampstead Theatre); *The Importance of Being Earnest, Beauty and the Beast, Alice in Wonderland* (Mercury Theatre); *Amma VR Experience* (Tara Theatre); *Death Drop: Back in the Habit* (Garrick Theatre/UK tour); *A Single Man* (Park Theatre); *The Importance of Being Earnest* (English Touring Theatre); *Bridgerton* (Secret Cinema).

Instagram: @bethduke_

Tian Brown-Sampson – Movement Direction & Intimacy Coordination

Tian Brown-Sampson (she/her) is a British-Caribbean theatre director, movement director, producer, writer, dramaturg, translator and facilitator. Her focus lies mainly within Black, East and South East Asian (ESEA), South Asian, and D/deaf and disabled theatre work within new writing, as well as promoting diversity, representation and accessibility on and off stage and in positions of power and leadership. Selected credits include: associate/movement directing/fight/intimacy: *Cymbeline* (Globe Theatre); *Makeshifts and Realities* (Finborough Theatre); *Possession* (Arcola Theatre); *Til Death Do Us Part* (Theatre503); *Two Billion Beats* (Orange Tree Theatre). Directing: *The Promise* (KCL); *The Lesson* (Theatre503); *Violet* (Pleasance Theatre); *babydyke* (Talawa, BBC Radio 4); *Bougie Lanre's Boulangerie* (Talawa Theatre); *Two Billion Beats* (Orange Tree Theatre); *In the Black Fantastic* (Southbank Centre); *For Her* 还装什么男子汉 (Chinese Arts Now Festival).

Associate/assistant direction: *Roots* (Almeida Theatre); *Passing Strange, Further than the Furthest Thing and Ivan and the Dogs* (Young Vic); *A Dead Body in Taos* (Bristol Old Vic, Wilton's Music Hall); *Moreno* (Theatre503); *Gin Craze!* (Royal & Derngate, Northampton); *Does My Bomb Look Big in This?* (Soho Theatre, Tara Arts); *Under the Umbrella* (Belgrade Theatre, Tara Arts); and *Forgotten* 遺忘 (Arcola Theatre).

Instagram: @tianshakira

Jasmin Meara Wall – Stage Management

Jasmin Meara Wall is a London-based stage manager who trained at LAMDA, graduating with a BA in Technical Arts for Theatre in 2024. Since graduating, her theatre credits include technical swing for *Anne Boleyn: The Musical* at Hever Castle, production manager production at Bridewell Theatre for *Alice by Heart* and stage manager for *Double Act* at Southwark Playhouse Borough. Various more from sound no. 2 to production management, she always enjoys being a part of the behind the scenes of theatre.

Instagram: @jasminstech

Velenzia Spearpoint – Communications Coordinator

Velenzia (she/her) is a freelance theatremaker and producer, also working across digital content, marketing and communications for theatre and the arts. She is the artistic director of the Bread & Roses Theatre and co-director of multidisciplinary arts festival, the Lambeth Fringe. Alongside this, she works across the UK with a variety of theatre companies, festivals and arts organisations, creating and collaborating in roles spanning direction, performance, production, and facilitation. Her practice focuses on interdisciplinary projects that centre queer, women-led and working-class communities. Recent credits include *Purdah* (Mind Out Theatre); *The Queen of Quex Road* (Bread & Roses Theatre); *Sad-Vents* (Edinburgh Fringe) and *The Unravelling Fantastia of Miss H* (UK tour).

Maeve O'Neill, Rua Arts – Project Management

Maeve (she/her) is an independent arts producer, establishing Rua Arts in 2018. Rua, meaning red the colour of blood, energy and life. Rua Arts offers project management, arts administration and mentoring for artists and arts organisations led by arts producer, Maeve O'Neill. Maeve is executive producer for Neon Dance, company producer for Simon Mole and co-director of Your Words Your World CIC. She is a facilitator on producing and recently contributed an essay in Aurora Metro's book *Feminist Theatre Then and Now*. Rua Arts co-productions include: *Dry Season* (national tour); *Chicken Burger n Chips* (Brockley Jack); *Poisoned Polluted* (The Old Red Lion); *The Diary of a Hounslow Girl* (two national tours); *Screwed* (Theatre503 2016).

www.ruaarts.earth Instagram: @RuaArts

Make Birth Better – Panel Discussion Partner

Make Birth Better is an organisation supporting both parents and professionals impacted by birth trauma, they offer a wide range of training and raise their voices through campaigning.

www.makebirthbetter.org

'Make Birth Better have always found art to be expressive of the range of voices and experiences that are impacted by birth and birth trauma. We are glad to see this experience – that many will resonate with – being brought to life and hope those impacted by birth feel seen and know support is available.'

Birthrights – Panel Discussion Partner

Birthrights is the leading authority on the human rights of women and birthing people during pregnancy and birth in the UK. They champion rights by supporting women and birthing people, training healthcare professionals, holding systems and institutions to account, and making visible diverse experiences of maternity care.

www.birthrights.org.uk

'At Birthrights, we believe that all women and birthing people should be able to exercise their right to make informed decisions about their bodies and care, and to do so free from discrimination, coercion and violence. That's why we are thrilled to support The Soon Life and its sensitive and true-to-life portrayal of a birth experience that will strike a chord for so many.'

Talawa is the UK's outstanding Black British theatre company. Our purpose is to champion Black Excellence in theatre, to nurture talent in emerging and established artists of African or Caribbean heritage and to tell inspirational and passionate stories, reflecting Black experiences through art like no other.

www.talawa.com

SOUTHWARK PLAYHOUSE
BOROUGH

Southwark Playhouse is all about telling stories and inspiring the next generation of storytellers and theatre makers. It aims to facilitate the work of new and emerging theatre practitioners from early in their creative lives to the start of their professional careers.

Southwark Playhouse engages people of all ages across its community by offering a range of drama related activities that promote learning and social cohesion. Each year they work with hundreds of people through a range of projects both in-school and as extra-curricular activities. Southwark Playhouse's Participation programme is predicated around the belief that involvement in the arts is a fundamental right for all, regardless of what stage they may be at, and provides benefits far beyond the immediately obvious that benefit the individual and the community as a whole.

At the start of 2023, Southwark Playhouse opened its second new theatre in Elephant and Castle. Southwark Playhouse Elephant houses two spaces: a reconfigurable auditorium that seats up to 310 people, and a youth and community space exclusively for the use of Southwark Playhouse's extensive community and participation work.

In November 2023, Southwark Playhouse celebrated its thirtieth anniversary. Over the last thirty years, the theatre has been showcasing innovative and engaging work by talented theatre artists and looks forward to continuing this in future years to come.

www.southwarkplayhouse.co.uk

Acknowledgements

Firstly, to Maeve. Thank you for being there from the very beginning to the very end with nothing but positivity and dedication to realising this production.

Sarah, thank you for holding me strong and for showing me that I can do hard things.

Joe, you are a perfect Alex. Thank you for all the birth-dates!

I am so grateful to the entire creative team. Sarah B (and little Winnie), Tian, Jasmin, Alex, Velenzia, Beth, Shannon, thank you for all your work.

To our doulas Nikita and Suzie, your insights to homebirth and birth in general have been invaluable.

Southwark Playhouse, Chris, Ebe, Jess, Emma, Lee, Fergus, Joe P and the entire team, thank you for giving our play a home.

Jules Haworth, Michael Buffong & David Gilbert, thank you for nurturing and championing my work.

Lavinia Serban, your dramaturgical feedback on early drafts gave me clarity and direction.

Callan McCarthy, your instant connection to the script and wonderful words of support propelled my play publication. I'm so grateful.

Thank you to Sian Carter, Becca Sealy, Judy Tither and the whole team at Methuen for helping me to realise my long held ambition to be a published playwright.

To my agent, Luke Speed, thank you for taking me under your wing.

Aneta Zwierzynska, thank you for making me feel like a dancer.

Thank you to all the crowdfunders who have generously supported the production:

Aileen O'Neill, Anna 'Russian' Ponomarenko, Jen Edmondson, Natalie Glass, Tom & Alice Stratton Sophie & James Besley, Will & Jenny Taylor, Robyn Stephenson, Daniel Bush, Anna Lawrence-Jones, Chris & Jo Clark, Simon Porter, Laurence & Carol Taylor, contactgecko, Julie Teal, Paul Burgess, Evy Loizou, Naomi Shoba, Holly Cullen-Davies, KORProductions, Ayesha Siddiqi, Caren Onanda and every anonymous donor.

Liz Berry, thank you for your beautiful poetry. The Republic of Motherhood holds a special place on my bookshelf.

Ashanti, Taja, Joe. You already know!

Mum. Thank you for teaching me how to be a mother.

Ed. I couldn't have asked for a better birth partner or a better life partner.

And to my Etta Rose and Juno Blue . . . I'd do it all again to get you two.

The Soon Life

For Ed

Characters

Bec, *early 30s, mixed-race, 40 weeks pregnant*
Alex, *early 30s, white, father of* **Bec**'s *baby*

Note on the text

/ indicates an interruption.

A Note on the play

The action takes place in **Bec**'s *open plan living room in the spring of 2020. The stage should resemble the home of a typical, mid-thirties couple living in London with a smattering of birth-related items like a birth ball, pregnancy books, a TENS machine, a Moses basket.*

Bec *is in labour throughout the play. This is her first baby. She is having a home birth.*

The experience of labour and birth varies greatly from woman to woman. Birth has several stages.

The first stage begins with the latent phase during which the cervix begins to dilate and contractions may be mild and irregular. The mother is typically able to stay active and engage in light activities such as walking, listening to music, watching television and eating little and often while managing her contractions. The latent phase can last for hours or even days.

The active phase comes next and is usually the point at which the midwife will arrive if the mother is having a home birth. Contractions during this phase become stronger and more frequent, but there may still be many hours to go.

Next, transition, during which the mother may experience a lull in labour referred to as 'rest and be thankful' when contractions slow down or become less intense, allowing her to re – energise briefly before the second stage: stronger contractions, an urge to push and, eventually, the birth of the baby. The third and final stage follows, ending with the delivery of the placenta.

*Generally, **Bec** tries to cope with the physical discomfort and pain of labour with breathing techniques and hypnobirthing exercises. She spends much of the play actively moving, pacing the living room, bouncing on the birth ball, rotating her hips. For the most part, she is trying to be calm, collected and measured. It is taking her a great amount of effort to appear this way. There will come a point in the play when she is unable to keep the mask up any longer.*

Scene One

A flat in London on an April day. There is a hallway and beyond, a living room with upholstery covered with thin, polythene sheets. There is a birth ball and an inflatable birthing pool which has been filled with air but not yet with water. Off stage, there is a kitchen, a bathroom and a bedroom with an ensuite.

The intercom buzzes. **Bec** *answers.*

Bec (*into intercom*)   If you've got a parcel, it's fine to leave it on the mat and, yeah, go.

Thanks.

Alex (*through intercom*)   It's –

Bec   And I'm not accepting any of the neighbours' deliveries right now. So, don't – just – yeah.

Bec *hangs up and makes her way to the kitchen to put the kettle on. She returns wearing noise cancelling headphones. Knocking can be heard at the door.*

The body achieves what the mind believes.

The body achieves what the mind believes.

My baby and my body know exactly what to do.

Three, two, one. Relax. Relax, Relax.

More knocking.

I trust my body.

I trust my body.

I trust my body because my body is fucking awesome.

Three, two, one. Relax. Relax, Relax.

Persistent knocking.

Alex *enters wearing surgical gloves, a disposable face mask plus a plastic visor-style mask over the top. He looks like something out of a PPE nightmare.*

Alex   Shit.

Alex *grabs a piece of paper from the console table by the door, speedily makes it into a paper aeroplane or scrunches it into a ball and gently launches it in* **Bec**'s *direction.*

Bec *turns to see* **Alex** *standing there. She rips her headphones off and screams.*

Alex   Shit! Sorry, sorry, sorry. It's me, Bec. It's me. I didn't realise –

Beat.

Alex   Hi.

Bec   '*Hi*'? Fucking, '*hi*'?

Alex   I knocked.

Bec   Are you fucking crazy?

Alex   Hold on. (*Goes to take the masks off.*)

Bec   Wait. Don't –

Alex   You can't hear me through all this.

Bec   Keep it on.

Alex (*removing the gloves*)   I said, I buzzed. Then I knocked. / You didn't –

Bec   That doesn't explain why you're here. I said keep it on. I don't know where you've been.

Alex   It's fine, I've been tested. I'm clear.

Bec   Are you sure?

Alex   You're massive.

Bec   I'm normal-sized. Why do you have that?

Alex   Compared to when I last – but, yeah. Suits you. What?

Bec   Why do you have that key?

Alex   It's the spare. From the plant pot.

Bec   You can't just go around using spare keys in the middle of a pandemic. Leave it here after, when – just leave it here.

Alex   You're the boss.

Bec   Again, why are you –

Alex   It's your due date, so –

Bec   So? You think that entitles you to show up.

Alex   And my running shoes.

Bec   Your running shoes?

Alex   Yeh, running, it's my one-outing-per-day exercise.

Bec   Whatever. Help yourself. But gel your hands before you touch anything and then you can go.

Alex   Okay.

Bec   Have you been on the Tube?

Alex   I walked.

Bec   Good.

Alex *goes to get his running shoes.*

Alex (*as he goes*)   I would've just bought new ones but these are – they're my shape. You can't buy that.

(*O/S*) You've been ignoring my messages.

Bec   Not ignoring. Just not replying.

Alex *re-enters.*

Alex   That's the same thing.

Bec   Sent you the final antenatal updates like we agreed. I thought the ones about how *I* am were veering off topic.

Alex   Right. What's with the hot tub? That can't be good for the baby.

Bec (*laughing to herself*)   Is that all?

Alex   No.

Bec   I don't think there's anything else of yours here. The first clear out was pretty brutal.

Alex   No, I mean, how have you been?

Bec   Pregnant.

Alex   Tired?

Bec   Charming.

Alex   Not in a bad way.

Bec   When is being tired a good thing?

Alex   You look like you did first trimester / with all that sickness –

Bec   Well, I'm in labour so, y'know.

Alex   What?

Bec   You can go now.

Alex   What did you say just then?

Bec   Forget it.

Alex   You're leaking.

Bec   I know.

Alex   It's trickl–

Bec   I know. It's fine.

Alex   What does it mean?

Bec   It means it's a good day to work from home.

Alex   Hold on. Has it started?

Bec   Yes, I just said that.

Alex   When?

Bec   You weren't listening.

Alex   No, you were doing that mousey thing with your voice again. / You didn't want me to hear.

Bec   What mousey thing?

Alex   Shouldn't you be sitting down or something?

Bec   It's best to move around actually. Maybe you should.

Alex   Thanks, but –

Bec   Off you go, then.

Alex   Why didn't you ring me?

Bec   I didn't know what to say.

Alex   The salient information would've been fine.

Bec   'Salient information'?

Alex   Some kind of indication, that it's happening.

Bec   You've never been great on the phone. You always sound like you're in a bad mood.

Alex   I find having private conversations in public awkward.

Bec   Maybe you should get rid of the phone function on your phone then.

Alex   Are you having / contractions

Sound of the kettle reaching boiling and clicking off.

Bec   Oh, my tea.

Alex   You're making tea?

Bec   Why's that funny?

Alex   You're in labour.

Bec   Officially, yeah. First stage.

Alex   So, I wouldn't have thought afternoon tea would be a priority right now.

Bec   It's a cuppa.

Alex   The baby's coming. And you're making tea.

Bec   Well, I better just make it a cup and not a whole pot.

Alex   It's great to know that labour only increases a woman's appetite for sarcasm.

Bec   Casual sexism isn't really what this situation needs.

Alex   I'm actually thinking of going out and coming back in again.

Bec   Good idea. Ring ahead this time. Or better still, don't come.

Silence for a while. **Bec** *breathes deeply through an uncomfortable sensation.*

Alex   How often's that happening?

Bec   Pretty spaced out.

Alex   Are they contractions?

Bec   I don't know.

Alex   You don't know?

Bec   I've never had one before.

Alex   From what I've heard, I'd say no.

Bec   Heard where? Who do you know who's given birth?

Alex   I've seen *One Born Every Minute*. Yeah, you'd know about it.

Bec   It's just a few twinges right now.

Alex   And that's better than a contraction?

Bec   The only thing you've missed is some Braxton Hicks and me trying to make myself some raspberry leaf tea, which is supposed to help soften the cervix / so don't give me any shit about afternoon tea.

Alex   Well, that's me told. I've got nowhere to go when you pull out the cervix card.

Bec   Why are you watching birthing shows?

Alex   Nothing else to do in lockdown. Have you called the hospital?

Bec   Not yet.

Alex   Shouldn't you let the midwives know you're coming, get on their delivery rota or whatever?

Bec   I think you're confusing this with Deliveroo.

Alex   It's not entirely dissimilar.

Bec   Don't make jokes.

Alex   You did.

Bec   It's the labour law. I can do whatever I bloody like.

Alex   Wow. Okay.

Bec   I've text Kate to let her know. So, just fucking relax. It's all fine.

Alex   Who's Kate? And there's something deeply unsettling about a heavily pregnant woman with a potty mouth.

Bec   From breaking and entering to bump shaming. You're on a roll.

Alex   What's bump shaming? / A new hashtag?

Bec   I get enough of that trying to get a coffee and the barista insisting on decaf for 'the baby's sake'.

Alex   They've got a point. And, I wasn't bump shaming. I'm just a bit worried about the baby picking up on all that negative energy. So, wait, *who's* Kate again?

Bec   Kate is my new midwife.

Alex   Another one?

Bec   And, on your previous point, I'm a grown woman, doing pretty well all things being considered, so I think I can be the judge of how much caffeine is good for my body and the one growing inside me as well as how I choose to express myself verbally. And anyway, swearing releases tension in the body and the mind. And releasing tension is all I'm about. Floppy face. Floppy fanny.

Alex   Come again?

Bec   Flop –

Alex   Actually, don't. Is that a saying?

Bec   Yes. Kate says it.

Alex   What happened to what's-her-name, Marie? Maria?

Bec   I switched to Kate after my thirty-six-week check-up. I was fed up with Ann-Marie's disapproving stare. She kept telling me I should hire a doula.

Alex   Dou-what?

Bec   Dou-*la*. Someone you can have at the birth, to support – things.

Alex   Isn't that what midwives are for?

Bec   No, it's separate. Like, emotional. It's not a medical thing. Forget it.

Alex   What, like, some kind of hippy? (**Bec** *scoffs.*) What? I've got nothing against hippies.

Bec   Anyway, Kate's fine with my plan.

Alex   What plan?

Bec Me getting on with things until she's free to come round.

Alex Is she picking you up?

Bec No, Alex. She isn't picking me up. She's just, she's coming round. To be here. To do everything –

Alex You're doing it here? Since when?

Bec I've been thinking about it for a while.

Alex How long's a while?

Bec Since a deadly virus started picking people off like flies. Sometime around then.

Alex And you didn't think you should let me know?

Bec Say that again in your head and see how it sounds.

Alex Bec, we broke up. I'm not dead.

Bec Like I need reminding.

Alex You can't do it here.

Bec Why not?

Alex It's a new carpet.

Bec It's not up to you. You don't live here anymore.

Alex But –

Bec Fuck the carpet.

Alex What if it affects the sale? (**Bec** *laughs with disbelief.*) What? Remember that flat in Crouch End? The estate agent let slip that the old guy had died in the downstairs loo and you made me withdraw the offer.

Bec Someone dying and someone being born is not the same thing.

Alex Is your cousin coming?

Bec   I feel like you're a bit confused about the whole concept of lockdown.

Alex   In lieu of sisters and with your mum stuck in another time zone, I thought the next best person would be Donna. I'm sure Matt Hancock would make an exception for that.

Bec   Why would I want my cousin to watch me giving birth? I wouldn't invite her to a smear test.

Alex   For fuck sake, Bec, / we don't have time for this.

Bec   Easy there, potty mouth.

Alex   So, not Donna. Then who?

Bec   Having anyone here, apart from my midwife, would be breaking the rules, technically.

Which begs the question why you're here. And spare me the running shoe crap.

Alex   I wanted to – I just thought – (*Pause.*) I'm doing a half marathon –

Bec   Time to go now, Alex.

Alex   So, the midwife is going to get here soon as, to sort this?

Bec   It doesn't work like that. But I can manage on my own / until she arrives.

Alex   On your own?

Bec   Did I stutter?

Alex   Have you lost the plot?

Bec   Do you want tea?

Alex   What? No. No, I don't want any tea right now, can you believe?

Bec   Okay. Okay.

Alex   This is fucking madness.

Bec   Now who's being dramatic?

Alex   I'm serious, Bec. This is next level. You can't sulk off and give birth on your own.

Bec   Who's sulking? I'm just getting on with things.

Alex   You should go to the hospital.

Bec   And you should go to wherever it is you're headed next.

Alex   No, I really, *really* think you should go / to hospital.

Bec   Dangerous places, hospitals.

Alex   Come on.

Bec   It's true.

Alex   You're being ridiculous. It's not too late.

Bec   Obviously. It's barely begun.

Alex   Look, I'm not trying to stress you out –

Bec   Speaking of 'too late'.

Alex   You need to review this plan you think you've got. You need someone with you. You need to be at the hospital, with someone. You need a birth partner, Bec.

Bec   It was you, Alex. Remember?

Beat.

Alex   Surely there's someone you can ask? One of the uni girls, someone from the antenatal course? Your hairdresser?

Bec   I'm having a baby. It's not a case of scrolling through my phonebook and picking someone I like, like I'm meeting them for a coffee. My whole body is going to open up and another person is going to climb out. Do you get that?

Silence for a while.

Alex   I might as well stay. Since I'm here.

Bec   What?

Alex   I'll stay.

Bec   No.

Alex   Just until the midwife arrives. / Then I'll leave you to it.

Bec   I'm not asking you –

Alex   You never ask, for anything, so, I'm proposing –

Bec   Not again / please.

Alex   Offering! I'm offering –

Bec   Clearly, the partner bit's already gone to shit. You want to try the birth requirement again too?

Alex   I know my knowledge of birth, birthing, is limited and mostly internet based, but it doesn't seem like something you should do on your own at any stage. I bet your mum isn't happy about this.

Silence.

Bec   What difference does that make? I'm here and she's stuck over there.

Alex   She knew the situation though?

Bec   You can't tell the Class of '84 anything about babies. They think they know everything.

Alex   I mean the situation. Us? (*Pause.*) Beccy!

Bec   I haven't found a good time to –

Alex   Bec!

Bec   Your mum fucking cried when you told her. / Why would you want to make my mum cry, Alex? Why?

Alex   It's been two months. You need to tell her we're not together anymore. Who have you told?

Bec   A group of strangers at pre-natal yoga. And you do not want me to repeat their thoughts on the matter.

Alex   You haven't told a single person you actually know?

Bec   Once the baby's here to distract them, it won't matter.

Alex   You've just been carrying it on your own?

Bec   Turns out this bump is a bit like Mary Poppins' handbag. Plenty of room for all kinds of shit.

Alex   Stubbornness doesn't wear off in labour then?

Bec   But, Alex, it's what you love most about me. Loved. (*Beat*.) Look, I appreciate your generous proposal, but I will be fine. I've got Kate on speed dial. I can ask Siri for help if I can't reach the phone. I told the girls at 114 I'd thump on the floor three times if I need them. I'm covered. You can go now, Alex. I don't want you here.

Lights.

Scene Two

Bec *is on the phone speaking to a midwife at the hospital.*

Bec   I've been drinking the tea and bouncing on the ball.

. . . Like, a tightening in my tummy that fades away after a few seconds. I felt a bit of fluttering this morning. It woke me up.

. . . Just breathing through them when they come. Is that –

. . . Paracetamol? For – That's not going to touch the sides, is it? Um, I guess, it is a bit like period pains . . . in a way.

(*Quickly*.) Could you just tell Kate about my progress and get her to call? She only replied to my first few texts but – so I just wanted to make sure –

. . . No, I know. It's just that I'm on my ow – Hello? Hello? Was I on hold then? What?

. . . Yes, I've got a TENS machine. And labour combs. Plenty of snacks.

. . . A boxset? No. Well, what are you watching at the moment? . . . No, never seen it –

. . . Okay, okay. Immediately. iPlayer. Fine. Sorry?

. . . Say – huh? Every time?

. . .. Now? But –

(*Timidly at first.*) Bring it on.

(*With the midwife's coaching, she becomes more defiant.*)

Bring it on. Bring it on!

Lights.

Scene Three

Alex *lets himself in with the key again. He begins to remove his jacket. A parenting manual falls out of one of the pockets.*

Bec   What the hell?

Alex   Where's the coat stand?

Bec   Don't make yourself comfortable. You've got your trainers. Why don't you try them out now?

Alex   I could hear you.

Bec   What?

Alex   You're out of breath. You're mooing.

Bec   You were listening?

Alex   Don't act like you've never done it.

Bec   That was one time.

Alex   You were the other side of the bathroom door and thought I was having a wank / and got really pissed off at me.

Bec   Who has a wank when their girlfriend's in the next room?

Alex   Anyway, I wasn't. I was having / a shit.

Bec   I remember the incident, thank you. Now, leave. I mean it.

Alex   I'll just sit in the corner.

Bec   No.

Alex   I don't want to / leave you –

Bec   Well, I don't particularly want to give birth, but we can't always have what we want.

Alex   I can help.

Bec   God, when I begged you to stay, you left. Now I want you to go, I can't get rid of you.

Alex   It hasn't been easy.

Bec   No, shit. It's been horrendous.

Alex   For either of us.

Bec   Not today, Alex. I'm not arguing with you today.

Alex   So, don't argue.

Bec   I know you probably expected me to call you and you'd come running back and get here to find me in a heap / on the floor –

Alex   You think I want you to be like that?

Bec   To need you, Alex. I don't.

Alex   You need someone. And like it or not, I'm the only one around.

Bec   This is hurting.

Alex   Contraction?

Bec   No. (*Pause.*) What if I decide to strip off and get into the pool – that's pool, not hot tub – before Kate arrives?

Alex   That's fine.

Bec   No it isn't. It's, no, it's –

Alex   I've seen it all before. That's how we got here.

Bec   There's no before anymore. There's only now.

Alex   It's fine.

Bec   For you maybe. No one's asking you to expose yourself. Why I am I always the one who has to do that?

Alex   We're losing sight of what we're really talking about here.

Bec   This is my birth.

Alex   It's the baby's birth.

Bec   But I'm the one doing it.

Alex   It's practically child abuse.

Pause.

Bec   Wow.

Alex   Not like, *child abuse* child abuse.

Bec   Wow.

Alex   In an ideal world, you'd let me get you a cab to the hospital. The next best scenario is, I stay, keep an eye on you / for a bit and

Bec   Keep an eye on me? / I'm a grown –

Alex   make sure you don't pass out, then the midwife can take over. It's not *completely* absurd.

Bec   It's not like I'm free birthing.

Alex   I don't know what that is.

Bec   When some badass women do it alone, no doctors, no one around. So, stop trying to make out that what I'm doing is extreme. I'm waiting for the midwife. She'll be here when I need her.

Alex   So I don't get a say this time either?

Beat.

Bec   And would you please stop using the word 'hospital'. That's the last place I want to be right now. There's more chance of me leaving there with more than I went in with.

Alex   Yeah, the baby.

Bec   And the rest.

Alex   This is ridiculous.

Bec   I want to have my baby then step into my own shower and climb into our – *my* – own bed, okay? This is going to be a positive experience, despite the people who've tried to tell me all about their own catastrophic deliveries or how their sister died for a few minutes before the baby arrived, or how their pelvic floors are now on the outsides / of their bodies.

Alex   Too much information.

Bec   This isn't going to be one of those. 'Start as you mean to go on.' Whoever said that was thinking about birth when – (*She experiences a strong sensation. It scares her.*)

Beat.

Alex?

Lights.

Scene Four

Alex *sits, out of the way, scrolling through his phone.* **Bec** *watches series 1, episode 1 of* Fleabag, *bouncing on the birth ball as Fleabag's 'pretty standard bouncing' line blares from the TV.*

Lights.

Scene Five

Bec *gets the pump for the gym ball*.

Alex   Thought I'd filled it to bursting when we bought it.

Bec   Just needs a top up. I'm always on it.

Alex   I'll do it.

Bec   Okay. Thanks.

Alex *tops up the gym ball*. **Bec** *picks up the book that fell out of* **Alex***'s pocket*.

Bec   *The Co-Parenting Guide*?

Alex   What?

Bec   You just carry this around?

Alex   I came from the restaurant. Had a bit of a clear out.

Bec   I didn't know we'd decided on an approach.

Alex   We haven't. I'm just getting my head round options.

Bec   With the help of the trusty *Co-Parenting Guide*?

Alex   It's not a great read to be honest.

Bec   I doubt it was destined to be top of the non-fiction chart.

Alex   The guy who wrote it is a class-A twat.

Bec   A kindred spirit.

Alex   He thinks he's written some kind of mystic text. Like he's the father of all the world's children. It's mostly bollocks. There's this other book I've been reading –

Bec   Reading *and* running.

Alex   What?

Bec   Nothing, just seems like you've got a lot of time on your hands.

Alex   I think everyone does at the moment.

Bec   It's a shame the hospitality industry didn't get furloughed sooner. (*Pause.*) Carry on, what other book?

Alex   By these two Scandinavian doctors with loads of kids. Basically, the Swedish von Trapps. They think parents should draw up a contract before the baby lands, to divide every responsibility equally down to the last second when it comes to the kid, the house. Everything.

Bec (*sarcastically*)   What a lovely notion. Is it a picture book? Are there unicorns too?

Alex   It's just an idea.

Bec   A bit ill-conceived maybe? No pun intended.

Bec *unwraps an energy bar and takes a bite.*

Alex   Are you supposed to eat while you're in labour?

Bec *chuckles to herself.*

Alex   Give me a break. I'm obviously a bit clueless on all the ins and outs of this. No pun.

Alex'*s phone rings.*

Bec   Who's that?

Alex   My head chef.

Bec   Do you need to take it?

Alex   No. (*He hangs up the call.*) He'll survive.

Bec   Look, you should probably try and think of this as the last event at the Reproductive Olympics. Everything an athlete does works in labour. Moving around, stretching, getting outdoors. Focus, deep breathing and calories. This is the arena, Kate's my coach, that's the pool. And at the end, instead of a medal, I win a baby.

Alex   Well, at least let me do the catering. I can make you something. (**Alex** *makes his way to the kitchen.*) Before we closed, I put a Bec-inspired dish on the menu.

Pause.

(*O/S*) Fridge is pretty bare apart from the biggest platter of sushi / I've ever seen. And the champagne we got for our –

Bec   Don't touch those! That's my post-birth celebration. I want them in my bump as soon as it's vacant.

Alex   Fish? (*He re-enters.*) You're vegan.

Bec   I *was*.

Alex   Oh.

Bec   I want a burger. A big one. . . Five Guys. Dirty. All the toppings. Fuck the lettuce wrap, I want buns. Double buns, a pair for each patty, but all in the same stack so that it's impossible to contain till it reaches your mouth. And chips. *The* chips! The Cajun ones they fill the bag with. And that *mayo*, all over them. Everywhere. The oiliest, eggiest – And then – Oh no, they don't do deserts, do they?

Alex   Peanut butter milkshake?

Bec   Or I could cheat on them with a McDonald's apple pie. What about you?

Alex   What?

Bec   Are you hungry?

Alex   Feel like I've just eaten *that*, thanks. Anyway, that's quite a specific craving and there's no Five Guys round here so maybe I can whip something up.

Bec   We just got one. A few weeks ago.

Alex   Five Guys? Right, I'm moving back in.

Bec   Fuck you.

Beat.

Alex   Fair play.

Loaded silence.

It's ready.

Bec (*sits on the gym ball, gently rocks and bounces, closing her eyes, taking deep breaths and humming softly. She rubs her belly and speaks to her bump*)   How you doing, you?

Alex   I'm –

Bec   Not you.

Alex   Sorry.

Bec   Ready to come out soon? Mummy's here. Waiting for you. Mummy's here.

Alex   We both are.

Bec   Who you gonna be, huh? (*Quietly.*) Who are we gonna be?

Alex   Bec –

Bec (*feels a contraction coming*)   Mmmmmmm.

Alex   Bec?

Bec   Water bottle.

He hands the water bottle to her, steps away behind her and watches her deal with the contraction. He steps closer but remains out of **Bec**'s *view. He spends several moments with hand outstretched deciding whether to touch her before it subsides.*

Bec (*she sips*)   One down.

Alex   Let me make you something up. Gnocchi?

Bec   From scratch?

Alex   When was the last time I fed you anything out of a packet?

Bec   I don't know if I've got all the / ingredients.

Alex   Leave it to me.

Bec   Can you make that sauce?

Alex   With the truffle oil?

Bec   Yeah.

Alex   Coming up.

Beat.

Bec   Alex?

Alex   Yes?

Bec   What do you tell people when they ask why we broke up?

Alex   Nothing.

Lights.

Scene Six

Bec *is off-stage in the bathroom. There is a bowl of gnocchi on the table.*

Alex (*typing into his phone, shouts*)   I've logged that last one, Bec. Lasted thirty seconds. The one before was twenty minutes ago.

Bec (*O/S*)   You don't need to do that.

Alex   There's an app for everything. Can't see a pattern yet. When's that supposed to happen? Bec? (*He peers around the lounge nostalgically.*)

Alex *looks at old photos of their past holidays on the wall.*

It's ready by the way. Hope you're still hungry.

Bec *enters. She sees the gnocchi on the table and vomits on the floor.*

Alex   Shit.

Bec   Could you just –

Alex   Shit.

Bec *vomits again in the same spot.*

Alex   I'll get –

Bec   This is normal. Kate said I might vomit.

Alex   How many times?

Bec   How should I know? It's the smell.

Alex   Shall I call her?

Bec   No, this is part of it. I can manage.

Alex   I'll get a cloth.

Bec   Don't look like that.

Alex   Like what?

Bec   You're doing that face.

Alex   What face?

Bec   Rabbit in headlights face. You're shitting yourself on the inside.

Alex   I'm fine.

Bec   I've expelled a bodily fluid and you look like you want to stop the world / so you can get off.

Alex   I just said I'll get a cloth for the sick, okay? I'm muddling my way through this much as you are.

Bec   I'm not muddling.

Alex   Never.

Bec   What's that supposed to mean?

Alex   Nothing.

Alex *goes to get the cloth. He comes back and cleans.*

Does that mean we've moved on?

Bec   Sorry?

Alex   You said you were in the first stage before but is this a – a progression?

Bec   No, I think this is still the latent phase. Cervix softening, surges coming as and when. It goes something like latent, active, transition, baby, placenta.

Alex   Surges?

Bec   Contractions. Surges – it helps reframe them. Don't you think contraction sounds like some kind of legal document?

Alex   It hadn't really occurred to me. 'Surge' makes me think of football.

Bec   That makes more sense.

Alex   Sergio . . . Aguero? He plays for Man City.

Bec   I did not know that. But now I do. And now, I'm probably going to think of him every time I have one. Cheers.

Alex   Might help. Best centre forward in Premier League history. There are worse people you could call to mind while you –

Bec   Don't –

Alex   Peter Crouch?

Bec   Stop it.

Alex   Boris Johnson?

Bec   You?

Alex   Let's stick to public figures.

Bec (*reluctantly*)   Patrick . . . Valance?

Alex   Doesn't do it for you, eh? Melania Trump?

Bec   Any Trump.

Alex   True.

Bec   Lee Stokes?

Alex   Who?

Bec   Old housemate Lee.

Alex   Lee? Lee! I completely forgot he existed until just then. What happened him?

Bec   DJ-ing kicked off he and bought a place in Ibiza or something.

Alex   Nice. Way to go, Lee. Always liked him.

Bec   No, you didn't.

Alex   I did.

Bec   You accused him of waiting outside the bathroom for me whenever I had a shower and told him that if he didn't move out, you'd tell the landlord he'd been using the wifi to access the dark web.

Alex   If anything, I'm grateful to the guy. Gave you the push you needed to move in with me.

Bec   We didn't move in together because of Lee Stokes. It'd been two years.

Alex   I can't remember what we were waiting for.

Bec   Me neither.

Bec *sends a text to Kate the midwife.*

Kate must be finishing off at another delivery.

Alex   What if it overruns?

Bec   It's not a board meeting. I don't know. They'll probably send someone else.

Alex   Or maybe I'll have to deliver the baby.

Bec   Only one person delivers a baby and that's the mother. I love how people are always trying to take credit for that.

Alex   I was joking.

Bec   Make yourself useful and dot a few of those (*Pointing at electronic tealights on the coffee table.*) around please.

Alex (*he does so*)   Feels like a date. A birth date. Birthday-t. Get it?

Bec   The dad jokes are coming along then?

Alex   That was a good one.

Bec   Almost made me throw up again.

Alex   Pretty weird date though. Huh? Come on?

Bec   Could you dim the lights?

Alex   How's that?

Bec   Yeah. Very romantic. (*Pause.*) Did you go on many, y'know, before lockdown?

Alex   What?

Bec   Dates.

Alex   No, too busy running and reading.

Bec   After all the drinking and shagging you mean?

Alex   There hasn't been anyone else, Bec.

Bec   Well, they've been queuing up round the block for me.

Alex   Yeah?

Bec (*sarcastically*)   There's an app actually. It's like Tinder but for heavily pregnant women, at their most hormonal, and insecure, and anxious and glowing and horny. I've been a very active user.

Alex   I'm sure you've got a very popular profile.

Bec   I have.

Alex I've been thinking about names.

Bec Right.

Alex I've got a couple to add to the shortlist if I'm allowed.

Bec You're allowed.

Alex So, how about Ga –

Bec No.

Alex I haven't said anything.

Bec You said 'Gah'. Hard gee sounds are unpleasant. Everyone knows that.

Alex I was going to say 'Gavin' if you'll give me a chance. For a boy obviously.

Bec Gavin. Gavin? Gav. No. What does it mean?

Alex I don't know.

Bec So you've chosen it because?

Alex Don't you think it sounds dependable? Sturdy.

Bec Your son has to be 'sturdy'?

Alex Sturdy Gavin. That's the kind of guy you want to employ. And he's a laugh. He's an all-round great guy. I wouldn't mind being considered sturdy myself.

Bec Too bad. Anymore?

Alex If it's a girl, I was thinking, maybe, Henrietta. (*He pulls out his phone and searches for the name's meaning.*)

Bec Henrietta?

Alex What do you think?

Bec Henrietta. Henrietta. I don't think I've never met anyone called Henrietta. It's a bit –

Alex We could shorten it to something?

Bec   I don't know.

Alex   Here, look it means 'ruler of the home'. That's pretty cool. Someone with leadership qualities.

Bec   I don't hate it. But I was thinking about just, waiting, matching a name to a face when I finally see a face.

Alex   Your call. You're better at that kind of thing than me anyway.

Bec   It'll be my first time naming a human being.

Alex   No, I meant – Never mind.

Bec *feels a contraction coming on. It requires her to stand still. She purses her lips, scrunches her eyes closed and uses all her concentration and strength to try to contain her discomfort, but it builds.* **Bec** *then quickly grabs her phone and plays a new track. 'Boss' by Little Simz plays.*

Bec   Towel!

Bec *signals to the towel which* **Alex** *throws to her. She gets down onto the floor and onto her hands and knees. Then, at the height of the contraction and the track, she buries her face into the towel and wails. It passes. She comes to.*

Alex   Did that help? Grime?

Bec   Kind of.

Alex   Yeh, I don't think elevator music is going to cut it. What's on the rest of your push playlist?

Bec   Push play – How do you –

Alex   My meditation teacher, his wife just had their second. Not that she pushed. C-section.

Too posh to push.

Bec   Really?

Alex She definitely is. His coaching gig seems to be doing well and she's pretty much landed gentry, so they're doing alright. She gave birth on the Lindo Wing.

Bec Another new hobby you've acquired since you left.

Alex I've always been interested in mindfulness.

Bec Maybe, from a distance. You do know that a caesarean is surgery, right?

Alex Okay.

Bec Something else to recover from when you've got months of sleep deprivation ahead / which actually happens to be a torture technique in some countries.

Alex Here we go.

Bec You said it was her second, right?

Alex Yeah / but point taken before you get really get stuck in.

Bec For all you know she had PTSD. Or maybe she'd had two, even three miscarriages and didn't want to leave anything to chance. Or, I don't know, maybe her first baby ended up in neonatal and she could only touch him through a plastic glove, in a plastic box, let alone hold him in her arms, feed him, change his nappy. Maybe she had to leave the hospital without the baby and walk through her front door kicking IT'S-A-BOY! cards off the mat and looking at all the dead flowers that had arrived while she'd been at the cot-side of the said baby, the one she'd just spent the best part of a year growing inside her. Or maybe, maybe she was just too posh to push. Yeah, maybe that was it. (*Beat*). Time to fill the pool.

Alex Good.

Bec What?

Alex Nothing.

Bec   The tap connectors and the hose are in the bathroom. Just stick them on and reel it into here. I'll shout for you to turn on the tap. Okay?

Alex *goes to get the hose and hands one end to* **Bec**. *He exits.* **Bec** *positions the hose in the pool.*

Bec   Okay.

Alex (*O/S*)   Bec?

Bec   Turn it on.

Alex (*O/S*)   They don't fit.

Bec   What? Just push them on.

Alex (*O/S*)   They don't fit. Are you sure – They're not going on.

Bec   What? No. No, n, n, n, n, n no, no, no, no. Try again.

Alex (*O/S*)   I have. Have you got any more?

Bec   No, of course I don't. Why would I have more? That's them. Fuck.

Alex *enters.*

Alex   Can the midwife bring a couple?

Bec   No, she can't. I got them online. It needs to be ready, I might need it soon.

Alex   I'll sort it.

Bec   I don't want you doing that. I need it to work.

Alex   Don't worry. I can cobble something together.

Bec   You're rubbish at DIY.

Alex   C'mon.

Bec   Remember those shelves you put up over the bed? Remember the books that fell on my head in the middle of the night, one by one. You're shit at it.

Alex   There's no such thing as a dad that can't do DIY.

Bec   Don't get ahead of yourself.

Alex   Trust me.

Alex *gets black gaffer tape and a hammer from the kitchen and goes back into the bathroom.*

(*O/S*) Okay. Hose still in?

Bec   Yeah.

Alex (*O/S*)   Ready.

Bec   Go for it.

The pool begins to fill. **Alex** *comes back.*

Alex   See.

Bec   Is it going to hold?

Alex   Should do. I'm gonna gaffer this connection too, just in case. (*He does. It feels like it goes on for ages, the sound of the tape ruining the atmosphere.*)

Bec   That looks . . . inviting.

Alex   Really think you'll notice when you're in the thick of it?

Bec   Probably not.

Alex   How's the temperature?

Bec   Nice. I mean, good. Thanks.

Silence.

Bec   Surge'd be good right now.

Alex   You *want* to have a contraction?

Bec   Anything's better than an awkward silence.

Alex   Actually, a contraction would be preferable.

They both laugh.

Bec   Or that playlist.

Alex   You really haven't made one? You were the one who told me that the answers to all of life's questions can be found in a song. A Sondheim song.

Bec   Sounds like something I'd say right after an audition, right before I hear I didn't get the job.

Alex   You get the job sometimes.

Bec   Sometimes. I've been doing a bit of DIY myself actually. Built the cot.

Alex   You?

Bec   Moi.

Alex   Super Mom.

Bec   And a new chest of drawers after I washed all the baby grows and –

Alex   I would've come round to help with stuff like that.

Bec   I didn't want to bother you.

Alex   The restaurant's still shut. We tried take aways but – It's simple, honest food. It relies on the setting, shared tables, the possibility that the person you're sitting next to might change your life, I don't know. It probably wasn't – I wouldn't have bothered with it all if – Wouldn't've been worth it.

Bec   What?

Alex   Everything. Anything.

Bec   It'll recover. It's a special place.

Alex   Thanks to your magic touches.

Bec   You had the vision for it.

Alex   I'd love to take her there one day. Get her cooking. Do you think she'll be a chef or a dancer?

Bec   Maybe they'll be something else entirely.

Alex   As long as she's happy.

Bec   She. He. They. Yeah.

Alex   So, what now?

Bec   More of the same. Can't just skip this bit in real life.

Alex   Have you heard back from Kate?

Bec   No, but, soon probably, so you might as well help me get a few last bits ready, before you – before she arrives.

Alex   I'll grab a bowl just in case you need to – again.

Bec   Good idea. And could you get the charger for the speaker? And the spray bottle that's by the side of the bed. And my hairband. The yellow one with the –

Alex   I know.

Alex *goes to the bedroom.*

Bec   Can you see my worry beads in there?

Alex   What?

Bec   The worry beads we picked up in Athens?

Alex   I thought they were an ornament.

Bec   No, I actually use them.

Alex *returns with all the items.*

Alex   Now, *that* was a trip.

Bec   Greece? Yeah. I think it might be my favourite place on earth.

Alex   Do you remember when we nearly moved there?

Bec   I remember.

Alex   It's funny how things turn out.

Bec   Funny. Devastating. Same thing I guess.

Alex   Are you always going to hate me?

Bec   There was me thinking I was the villain of the piece. But I suppose you left, so.

Alex   I left? You lied. That's why I left.

Bec   Secrets aren't lies, Alex. They're secrets. Not intended for others.

Alex   That's not the kind of thing you keep a secret.

Bec *puts her coat on. Beat.*

Bec   Keep an eye on the water. There's a fill line at the side.

Alex   Where are you going?

Bec   For a walk.

Alex   You can't just go walking around out there. In labour.

Bec   That's exactly what I'm going to do. Plod myself around the green for ten minutes.

Alex   I'll come with you.

Bec   No. Stay here. Check in with your parents or something. Tell them the *salient* information.

Alex   I've already text Dad.

Bec   Then just wait. Or, I don't know.

Alex   Okay, but if you're not back in exactly ten minutes, I'll start to worry.

Beat.

Bec   Remember when you had to go to Cape Town for that event and I'd just started a temp contract between shows, so I couldn't go with you?

Alex   Yes.

Bec   Remember how we said we wouldn't text or call, we'd just write, cos we thought it'd be romantic, old skool? That night you landed – more like a week, actually – we just stayed in bed until we thoroughly un-missed each other. We talked. Talked like we were really listening. Like we'd only just met. Like we'd never see each other again.

Alex   I remember.

Bec   Why don't you try to think of me being away from you now, like that? Or better still, think of it like the last two months when we've really been apart, despite being in the same city. Broken apart. No, 'I'm sorry this is happening, I can't wait to be a parent with you, let's get back together'. Think of the next ten minutes like that, and you'll be fine. And don't touch my sushi. Not a single nigiri.

Bec *exits.* **Alex** *kicks the wall. He groans, like he is in pain. Like he is having a contraction. The pain passes. He composes himself. He goes over to the speaker, pairs and starts to make a push playlist for* **Bec.**

Lights.

Scene Seven

Bec *is flicking through The Co-Parenting Guide.* **Alex** *is testing the water temperature in the pool.*

Bec   How's everything going to work?

Alex   I don't know. We didn't get that far.

Bec   Do you think we need to formally agree on something?

Alex   That would probably be sensible. When I can come round, how often, that kind of thing.

Bec   What were you thinking?

Alex   I want to help out with night feeds.

Bec   How's that going to work?

Alex   I could prep bottles, take turns doing some of the night wakes. I don't know. I don't know. I just want to be there when –

Bec   There's something about the night. Makes everything feel sore to the touch. Don't you think?

Alex   Bec.

Bec   Kind of wish the sun / was still up now actually.

Alex   Look, what if I take the sofa a night or two a week?

Bec   I'm not sure. Don't want to muddy the water or anything. Plus when the baby's here I'm going to be even more irresistible to other men, what with all the lactating and vomit stains and all, so. (*Pause.*) It was a joke.

Alex   I'm doing my best to find it funny.

Bec   By the way, I need to FaceTime my mum at some point and, I think it would be – I need you to, feature in it. You don't have to say anything, but, I need her to see you, so she doesn't worry.

Alex   I'm not participating in a staged video call.

Bec   It'll only last / for a few minutes.

Alex   I'm not doing that.

Bec   Please.

Alex   What if I hadn't shown up?

Bec   I don't need to answer that because, here you are. It's the least you can do considering you walked out on me.

Alex   It's like you enjoy the way that sounds.

Bec   I'm stating a fact.

Alex   What has she got to say about you having a home birth?

Bec   She thinks it's a bit 'earth mama' but I've told her my reasons.

Alex   And she's okay with it?

Bec   She said it's up to me. She had me in the toilets at Wimpy, remember, which she said she wouldn't wish on anyone so in a way I think she's happy for me. (*Beat.*) I wish she was here. I've been talking to her more lately, like this rush to get to know her more than I have at any other point in my life. She's been telling me all these stories about being a single mum. Finding out she was pregnant with me the day after my dad died.

Alex   I didn't know that.

Bec   Me neither. I nearly called you to tell you. I dialled and everything.

Alex   You should've let it ring. (*Beat.*) Are you nervous?

Bec   No. Mild tokophobia maybe, but –

Alex   Fear of TikTok dance routines?

Bec   Fear of giving birth.

Alex   That's an actual phobia?

Bec   Yes.

Alex   But isn't it what you do?

Bec   Who? Me?

Alex   Women generally, I mean.

Bec   Oh, so, just because ecologically –

Alex   It's bio / biologically.

Bec   Whatever – because women are *bio*logically designed to give birth, that means I shouldn't be, in any way, scared of what's happening right now?

Alex   Well, I keep hearing all this stuff about artificial wombs. Baby bumps might become obsolete.

Bec   Your daily dose of *Woman's Hour*?

Alex (*sheepishly*)   Not every day.

Bec   I was completely joking. (*Sarcastically.*) You don't seem to be coping too well with lockdown, Alex. I'm concerned.

Alex   You're taking the piss, but I think it's important for people to expose themselves to new ideas. I thought you'd be all for it.

Bec   You banned me from listening to it in the car whenever we happened to be making a journey somewhere between 10 and 10.45am. It's just weird how you've done a one-eighty.

Alex   I've been trying to understand, Bec. Why you didn't tell me. Why you did it, I guess.

Bec   Well, congratulations. Only two months too late.

Quiet.

Alex   Before, I meant, are you nervous about meeting her?

Bec   Her?

Alex   Yeah, I keep imagining she's a little girl. With my labyrinthine ears and your lips. Not the look of them exactly, but the feeling. Y'know what I mean? The feeling they convey.

She'll love music. She won't mind about dad dancing. She'll love it, dancing with me. And with you, at her birthday parties and weddings. We'll listen to classical in the mornings and Bruce Springsteen in the afternoons, and stand in front of the mirror, her in my arms, her arms around me. And if she's ever scared of anything, I'll get her to tell me what it is and I'll turn it into a funny story and she'll laugh until she's not scared of it anymore, only bemused, happy again and maybe, yeah, maybe that's how she'll go through life a little bit.

And we'll go places. I won't just take her anywhere. I'll take her everywhere.

She'll ask me all kinds of questions and sometimes I'll know the answers and sometimes I won't. She'll challenge me and surprise me in ways I never thought possible. She'll hate the way I get her to text me whenever she arrives at a mate's house, or when she's getting the bus home late. But, that'll probably never happen, cos I'd drop everything to come and get her in the car at 2am when her battery's about to die and she's had enough of sneaking into bars on a Friday night and just wants to curl up in her own bed. Then she'll come downstairs in the morning to black pudding on toast and cups of tea. Cos she'll definitely be a foodie, Bec. Y'know? She'll try anything once. She'll be brave and she'll crave adventure. She'll be a Brownie. No, she won't, she'll be a scout. A cadet. Whatever a boy can do. She'll be whatever she wants to be and won't let anyone tell her she can't.

She'll become a start-up CEO and probably invent something we all really need but haven't thought of yet. And she'll be so kind. Good. Like *really* good. And not in a self-gratifying way. She won't take thanks for it. She'll just have a good soul. She'll be good people.

I'll get her into coding and take her to football training. We'll get season tickets and make up new chants while we eat chips and wrap our scarves round our necks so we don't see our breath during those frosty games in the middle of the season. She might ask about us and I'll tell her how we met, when you asked me the time on the Tube and we ended up going all the way to the end of the Bakerloo line together because we couldn't stop talking. And one day she'll tell me she's found someone. Someone she really likes. She'll think she's fallen so hard that she'll never want to be with anyone else. She'll only be twenty-one but she'll believe she's in love and she probably will be. I'll tell her that there's nothing like it and if she feels it, she should hang on to it.

Then maybe one day I'll get to do the father of the bride speech on her wedding day and I'll have all these anecdotes about her as a little girl and then a teenager and then the beautiful woman I've just walked down the aisle. And we'll dance again like we used to when she used to fit in my arms, when she used to curl up and fall asleep on my chest.

And then she'll be someone else's to look after.

Long pause.

Bec   Sounds like a lucky girl.

Alex   If she takes after you, she will be.

Bec *looks at him until it becomes too revealing to maintain eye contact for a second longer.*

Bec   I should probably mention, there's a letter on the console table, if anything happens.

Alex   I –

Bec   What?

Alex   I think I might've made it into a paper aeroplane.

Bec   Alex.

Alex   That was the signal, that I was here. It was the closest thing I could grab.

Bec   Well, could you please unmake it into a paper aeroplane and put it back where you found it?

Alex *picks up the paper.*

Alex   What do you mean 'if anything happens'?

Bec   It's for the baby. In eighteen years. Give it to the baby for me.

Alex   Where will you be?

Bec   Don't make me say it. You know what I'm talking about.

Alex   You think –

Bec   It's a possibility.

Alex   I knew it. Let's get you to some doctors. Machines. Pain killers. All the needles.

Bec   Slow down, Professor Whitty. This has nothing to do with the fact that I'm doing it here. It's just isn't something you can take for granted.

Alex   It's 2020.

Bec   That just makes it easier to Google all about women who have lost too much blood or developed septicaemia or, I don't know. And I'm mixed race, so.

Alex   So?

Bec   It makes things harder. Worse. No, different. It's different for me.

Alex   Different how? Different racially?

Bec   Yes, different as in three times more likely to die doing this than white women. As if it wasn't hard enough.

Alex   I get how that must make you feel but –

Bec   People choose to listen less when they want to, depending on who's speaking.

Sometimes. That's all. And going by the lack of response from the midwifery team, I'm starting to wonder if they can hear me.

Alex   Wait, the midwives / are (*Unspoken: racist too.*) –

Bec   Just to remind you, this baby we're having is mixed-race too, so be very careful.

Alex   I'm fully aware of that, and you were there when I set my parents straight after all that caramel-coloured crap at Christmas.

Bec   I should fucking hope so too.

Alex   I'm on your side, okay? (*Pause.*) If I came across anything less than . . . well, I didn't mean to. (*Pause.*) They genuinely can't wait to meet her. They're going to love her so much. They already do. It's their first grandchild. (*Beat.*) They miss you. (*Silence.*) I said they –

Bec   I heard you.

Quiet.

Alex   I've had a lot of time to think about things. The way I reacted.

Bec   Don't.

Alex   I want to explain.

Bec   We don't need to rehash it. I can't do it again.

Alex   I'm not trying to rehash anything. I just need you to know, because I've had the chance to think about how it all went and how I found out. It was a mixture of things, I think, a mixture of – I felt like I didn't have a choice.

Bec   You had a choice.

Alex   I was angry.

Bec   You chose to leave.

Alex   I tried to come back, remember?

Bec   You thought you could just un-leave me because there's a pandemic all of a sudden?

Alex   At least I tried.

Bec   A lockdown roomie wasn't really what I was after, thanks.

Alex   You don't know how angry the whole thing made me.

Bec   Not the whole thing. Me. I made you angry.

Alex   What you did made me – and the fact that I probably never would've found out if it hadn't been for that slip up.

Bec   Slip-up? Right, yeah. I'd call it an utter breach of patient confidentiality which destroyed our relationship. But, yeah, 'slip-up' works too.

Alex   So, you still don't think what you did destroyed our relationship?

Bec   You obviously do by the sounds of it.

Alex   I've been trying to understand it.

Bec   Say it.

Alex   What?

Bec   You should be able to. What did I do that made you so angry you couldn't bear to be with me? Say it.

Alex   I'm not –

Bec   There are lots of words to choose from.

Alex   This isn't a game, Bec.

Bec   Termination.

Alex   Leave it. This isn't good for –

Bec   Feticide. Not as popular, that one.

Alex   You didn't think I deserved to have a say.

Bec   Or good, old-fashioned 'abortion' then.

Alex (*almost in spite of himself*)   And I'm not even sure you regret it.

Bec   It was my call to make. That's the truth, Alex. And maybe that makes you feel powerless and that's really what made you angry.

Beat.

The girl who used to serve me at the café once asked if this was my first and it felt like I was lying when I said 'yes'. I should've said, no, not really. Not exactly. There was one before, that I couldn't go through with because, I wasn't ready, we barely knew each other, so I made a call. I wanted to give *us* a chance. Just us. (*Pause.*) I'm ready now though. I am. And I'm happy in so many ways. But I also feel so fucking bad inside that I wonder if I even deserve this child. They should be someone's little brother or sister and I prevented that. I stopped that from happening because I told myself I was too fucking busy sending emails and dancing. But I was just scared. Every time I catch sight of myself in the mirror I feel a little bit of sadness. But, no, I don't regret it. I don't regret it any more than I do keeping this baby. This is our baby. Do you still love me?

Alex   You're carrying my child.

Bec   Not for much longer. What about then? When I'm not anymore.

Alex   You'll be the mother of my child.

Bec   The kind of love you had for me before. Do you still have that?

Alex   It's okay for it to be a different kind of love.

Bec   But it'd be nice to have something of our former selves left after tonight. Wouldn't it?

Beat.

Alex   There's no half marathon. It got cancelled. I didn't come back for my trainers.

Bec (*she begins to cry*)   I've hated doing those NCT classes on my own. I count the hours while the midwife tells us how to deal with unexplained crying in babies and all I can think is, what about me? What about unexplained crying in me? And consequently I now have no idea how to construct a swaddle or what to do if the umbilical gets – (*She stops abruptly. Feels her bump anxiously.*)

Alex   What's wrong?

Bec   When was my last contraction?

Alex   I don't know.

Bec   Check the app.

Alex   I think I've missed some.

Bec   They've stopped. I need to –

Alex   Calm down.

Bec   This is your fault.

Alex   Do your breathing.

Bec   Don't tell me what to do.

Alex   I'm trying to help.

Bec   What would help is some oxytocin.

Alex   Okay, I'll get some from the pharmacy? What does it look like?

Bec   You can't buy it. You make it. Things stimulate it in your body. I need stimuli.

Alex   Tell me what to do. Rub your back? What?

Bec   My nipples.

Alex   You're having me on.

Bec   That's the most effective area.

Alex   I can't –

Bec   I'm saying it's okay.

Alex   I can't.

Bec   Why?

Alex   I don't know. It's a can of worms. If I touch you –

Bec   I'm asking you to.

Alex *moves closer. He extends his hand towards her.* **Bec** *takes his hand and places it inside her top on her bare breast.*

Lights.

Scene Eight

Bec's *contractions have properly resumed. She is now using a TENS machine to manage the pain. She sings the first verse of Lauryn Hill's 'To Zion' singing her own name Beccy in place of Lauryn.*

Beat.

Bec   Do you really think they can really hear us?

Alex   They start hearing their first sounds around eighteen weeks in utero.

Bec (*playfully*)   Oh. In utero, really?

Alex   What? Why are you smiling?

Bec   Nothing, just tell me more about what goes on in utero. Sounds very anatomical. Like you've inhaled another book.

Alex   Just my way of getting to know my kid.

Bec   In utero.

Alex   Alright. Alright.

Bec   Sounds like it's in the Maldives. I want to book a flight.

Alex   Maybe I'll take you one day.

Bec   Oh, you've been, my friend and I'm not sure you'll be going back.

The joke they thought they were sharing dies.

Bec   When was eighteen weeks? Before we –

Alex   Yeah. Before.

Bec   That's something. At least they got to hear us, our old voices.

Alex   It gets stronger from then. They can hear everything. Even sounds we don't.

Bec   Did we shout a lot? I can't remember.

Alex   Yeah, a bit.

Bec   None of the neighbours knocked.

Alex   This is London. People don't interact with their neighbours unless there's a fire or you've got their Amazon parcel. Otherwise all you get are hard stares.

Bec   Got a few hard stares, did you?

Alex   One or two.

Bec   I've been singing to Bump every day. I do a mixture of up-tempo crowd pleasers and classic nursery rhymes. Any requests?

Silence.

Alex   Actually, do you mind if I talk to her?

Bec   Who?

Alex   The baby.

Bec   Go ahead.

Alex   Alone?

Bec   Pardon?

Alex   In private? If that's okay?

*He gestures to **Bec**'s headphones. She reluctantly puts them over her ears. She leaves a sneaky gap so she can hear what **Alex** says but this should not be obvious. **Alex** kneels down so his mouth is bump height. He gently brings his fingertips to **Bec**'s bump. He may even turn his ear towards the bump to see what he can hear.*

Alex   Hi. It's me. I know you haven't heard my voice lately and before that, it probably didn't sound very nice some of the time. Sorry about that. It wasn't your fault. I've missed you, even though I don't really know you yet, which is pretty cool. Not sure how everything's going to pan out after tonight. I know that opening another restaurant after your fiancée tells you they're pregnant probably wasn't the smartest move. Probably didn't help on top of everything else. I haven't felt very smart or parent-like lately. Wonder when that's supposed to kick in. I've let you down. Not being here. I should've been at all the classes with your mum. Should've worked out how to do, be – better – before you got here. Too late now. Do me a favour, while you're in there. Let her know how amazing she is. I think what she's done, growing you and keeping you safe, getting you ready and everything, is the most incredible thing I've seen anyone do.

Bec *gently touches* **Alex**'*s chin and guides him up to standing. She slides the headphones away from her ears. They linger. His hands still pressed against her bump, hers against his face. They are quiet. Slowly, they move their faces towards each other. They almost kiss.*

Lights.

Scene Nine

Bec'*s waters have broken. She phones her midwife. It goes to voicemail.*

Bec   Kate, things are ramping up now. I really, really need to hear from you . . . I've had the Hollywood gush, mucus plug and the kitchen sink. Everything. Everywhere. So, please get here . . . Something is happening – that I can't come back from . . . Please call me. Or just get here. Soon. I'm –

She hangs up. **Alex** *enters.*

Alex   Shit.

Bec   Is getting real.

Bec's *phone rings.*

Bec   Kate? . . . Who? . . . Wait, hold on? Alex, I can feel another –

She hands **Alex** *the phone. She stands in the doorway, pressing her back up against one side of it and stretching her arms out in front, pushing against the other side of the door frame. She uses the counter-pressure to help her cope with this surge.*

Alex   Hi, how far away are you? Her con – surges – are really close together, her waters have broken. It's time, right? Do you need directions?

He listens intently to the midwife's next reply which lasts for a minute or so. During the course of this, his face and demeanour change. He is at once crestfallen, conflicted, relieved and terrified.

Is this Kate I'm speaking with? . . . No. Kate. Kate *Something*, her midwife? She's supposed to be . . . No, no don't tell me to call an ambulance. She doesn't want – Wait, I'm trying to take this in. That can't be the only –

. . . What do you mean redeployed? . . . Staff shortages are what they have at Waitrose on a bank holiday. She's about to have a child. You can't expect me to tell her that the only person she's looking forward to seeing tonight more than the baby, has been called to another birth, somehow more important than this one, and that you want an ambulance to take her to her least favourite place and, that all the drug free hours she's already had were a complete waste of time?

. . . Yes, I do. Of course, I think it's the best place for her. But it's not about me. Or you.

. . . C'mon.

The phone goes dead.

Bec.

Bec   I heard. Fuck. Fuck, fuck, fuck, fuck, fuck.

Alex   They think an ambulance –

Bec   No! That's not what I wanted.

Alex   I don't know what to do.

Beat.

The birthing pool begins to overflow. **Alex** *rushes into the bathroom to turn the water off.* **Bec** *starts to panic.*

Alex   It's okay. It's all gonna to be okay.

Bec   This wasn't how it was supposed to go.

Alex   We'll figure it out.

Bec   This is the worst birthday I've ever been to. I'm not going to the hospital, Alex. I'm not. I'm not. I'm not going. I can't. I'm not going. / They can't make me.

Alex   Give me Kate's number. Maybe she can coach you, over the phone? I don't know.

Bec   How's that going to work?

Alex   Kate needs –

Bec   Fucking, fuck that fucking fucker, Kate. I've been dubious about Kate since I met her. Since she asked me if she could live stream the birth on her Instagram.

Alex   What?

Bec   She wants to go freelance or something. Trying to build her customer base. I never thought birthing from home could be bought and sold, but there you go.

Alex   Okay, okay. I'll to go forty-one. She's a doctor, isn't she?

Bec   Paediatrician.

Alex   That'll do. Does she still live there?

Bec   Don't know. Think so.

Alex   It's worth a try.

Bec   No, no, no. No. Don't leave me.

Alex   I won't. I'm not. I'm not, okay? I promise, I'll be right back.

Alex *exits.*

Bec (*to her bump*)   I'm sorry. I'm so sorry. I'll make it up to you. You're my soulmate.

Bec *takes the TENS pads off. She removes her dressing gown. She climbs into the pool. She switches between humming and lyrics in between deep breaths, gritted teeth and cries of pain. She changes position several times in the pool. She settles facing outwards, on her knees with her forearms resting on the rim of the pool and her chin resting on her hands.*

Bring it on. Bring it on. Bring it on . . .

Alex *knocks.*

Bec   Alex?

Alex   It's me.

Bec   No shit. Where's your key?

Alex   You made me leave it on the console table.

Bec   But I'm in the pool now.

Alex   Well, can't you just –

Bec   Are you joking?

Alex   Okay, don't – I've got this. I'm coming in.

Bec   No, don't –

With several loud blows, he busts the lock and breaks back into the flat.

Bec   Alex!

Alex   It doesn't matter. I'll fix the door later.

Bec   Where is she?

Alex   No answer. She must be at work.

Bec   At the hospital. Ironic. This is a shit show.

Alex   You got in [*the pool*].

Bec   It's helping.

Alex   I'm going –

Bec   Go on. Go! It's what you do best.

Alex   I'm *going* to ring the hospital. I'll speak to someone else. Tell them what's happened. Make them send someone else, so you have this. I want you to have this.

Beat.

Bec   Oh no.

Alex   What is it?

Bec   I think I –

Alex   What?

Bec   I want to push.

Alex   What? Why?

Bec   I don't know.

Alex   You can't.

Bec   God, I want to push.

Alex   You didn't a minute ago. / Sorry –

Bec   Fuck you, I have to.

Pause.

I'm going to – I can't stop– I have to – be sick.

Alex *takes off his shirt and kneels at the side of the pool.*

Alex   Bec –

Bec   Don't.

Alex   I've fucked up.

Bec   Doesn't matter.

Alex   How –

Bec   Fix it.

Alex   How –

Bec   Try.

Alex   Are you feeling?

Bec   I – I –

Alex *is transplanted to the rug at the centre of the room. His trousers and fly are now unbuttoned.* **Bec** *comes out of the bathroom. She is no longer pregnant. She is naked. She lays down next to him.*

Alex   Better?

Bec   So weird. Have I eaten anything off today?

Alex   Nothing I haven't had too. C'mere.

She nestles into **Alex***'s 'nook'. They hold each other for a while. He kisses her on the head.*

Alex   Too much jiggling around.

Bec   Oh God.

Alex   What's wrong?

Bec   Did you just call it jiggling / around?

Alex   Yeah?

Bec   Please don't call it that ever again.

Alex   Doesn't do it for you? A bit of jiggery pokery?

Bec   Stop it. Or it'll be the last jiggery pokery you ever get from me.

Alex   Too much fucking around then. Must've knocked that tofu steak for six.

Bec   Fucking around. That's better.

They kiss. Quiet. Then 'Help Me Lose My Mind' by London Grammar feat. Disclosure starts to play on the speaker.

Bec   Did you cue this?

Alex   Not my doing.

Bec   How did this become our tune again?

Alex   You claimed it for us.

Bec   Me?

Alex   At that bar. How have you forgotten this? You took my drink out of my hand, dragged me to the other side of the bar and said if I didn't enjoy what was about to happen, you'd buy me dinner.

Bec   I must've been wasted. I was right though, wasn't I?

Alex   I think I would've put up more of a fight if I'd known you were a professional [*dancer*] at that point.

Bec   It was cute, the way you tried to keep up. *Really* tried. (*She stifles a laugh.*)

Alex   Okay, thanks. Yeah, I was definitely the student and you were definitely the teacher in that scenario.

Bec   Don't be jealous. You've taught me plenty.

Alex   Could you just put that in a voice note so I have evidence of this?

Bec   Calm down. Okay. No. I don't know everything. Sometimes I think I don't know anything. Anyway, it keeps our relationship fresh.

Alex   Was it in danger of going stale?

Bec   Every relationship is in danger.

Alex   Deep.

Bec   True.

Beat.

Alex   Taught you a few things, have I?

Bec   Being naked always makes me a soft touch. Don't make me get dressed.

Alex   Naked Bec's my favourite. She's not as stubborn as the other one.

Bec   Oh, what? One of my best features, stubbornness. It's probably why you love me so much.

He kisses her on the head again. Quiet.

You don't think we've . . . No.

Alex   What?

Bec   We've . . . Oh God, what if we have?

Alex   What?

Bec   I can't say it.

Alex   C'mon.

Bec   Maybe.

Alex   I doubt it.

Bec   We might have. I ovulate around now.

Alex   I'm fairly certain we haven't conceived within an hour of having sex for the first time in our relationship without a condom.

Quiet again.

Bec   Maybe that's why I puked. Fuck, that's why I puked. I'm pregnant.

Alex   Bec, you're not pregnant.

Bec   Okay.

Silence.

I feel like we shouldn't've called it fucking around if we've just made a baby. That seems wrong now / to call baby-making fucking.

Alex   Chill out. We've got plenty more fucking baby-making to do. Months, maybe. And I can't wait. Hope so anyway. I need the buffer.

Bec   Buffer?

Alex   Yeah. It's only been a few days since we decided to stop stopping it from happening.

I'm still getting used to the whole idea. (*Pause.*) Got a few more pipe dreams I'd like to have a crack at before mini-me comes along.

Bec   I love a pipe dream. Tell me.

Alex   Okay but don't get angry, okay? Another restaurant. Solo this time. And maybe a, a, cookbook.

Bec (*smiling*)   Not angry.

Alex   Really?

Bec   Course not. 'Specially when I think back to what you were doing when we met. You were miserable / wearing the corporate hat.

Alex   I hated it.

Bec   So, go for it.

Alex   Yeah? Yeah. Maybe. I'll think about it.

Quiet again.

Bec   God, speaking of awful jobs, did I ever tell you I did medical role play while I was training? That was my worst job *ever*. Ever. Ever.

Alex   Don't think so.

Bec   I swore I'd never do it again even if it was 150 quid a day.

Alex   Sounds like quite a good earner.

Bec   I remember the worst case I had to play was a patient who was forty-one weeks pregnant.

So, basically, I'm pretending to go to the doctors for a check-up, wearing this massive pregnancy belly, this sandbag stitched into a vest and I – as the character, the patient – I tell the trainee GP, how I haven't felt the baby kick that day. Just, really casually. And that I'd been washing baby grows and getting ready for the now, overdue arrival of my baby slash sandbag, that I couldn't remember the last time it *had* kicked. But also how I hadn't thought anything of it, because sometimes babies fall asleep in the womb. Well, every day in fact. Just like we go to sleep at night, or take a nap during the day, babies do too. They sleep before they're even born. Did you know that?

Alex   Makes sense.

Bec   So, I'm there in my baby-bump-sand-bag costume, looking very fetching, and it turns out that the correct way for the student to handle the case – because they're doing this in front of an examiner – did I mention that?

Alex   Nope.

Bec   This all-seeing, all-knowing, Gandalf of the GP world, who's been a doctor for the last hundred years, and he's marking the wannabe GP on their performance in this very odd, fake GP surgery.

Alex   I can picture it now.

Bec   Don't joke. It's very intense. So, there I am thinking, I'm definitely being under paid for this shit because I have to play the same case twenty-six times in one day. Like *Russian Doll*. I just kept knocking on doors, sitting down in uncomfortable chairs, with this huge, fake belly, pretending to be happy, completely unsuspecting that there was only one correct way for these poor fuckers to deal with this kind of patient – an overdue, pregnant woman who says the words,

'I haven't felt the baby kick today.'

That was my opening line, by the way, twenty-six times.

'No, I haven't felt him kick today, Doctor, but he's probably just asleep. Oh, did I mention he's a boy? We found out. We couldn't wait.'

I try not to go off on a tangent –

Alex   You? Never.

Bec   I try not to be too disturbed by the fact that I can see the colour drain from the face of each and every trainee GP sitting across after my opening line as they try not to look at the examiner, the one who decides whether or not they'll get to do the job they've trained to do for the past decade.

Alex   What was the answer?

Bec   It –

Alex   Go on, I can't take / [*the suspense*]

Bec   It was dead. (*Pause.*) My baby had died.

Alex   Fuck.

Bec   They were supposed to tell me. No bullshit, then and there. My baby was dead.

Alex   How many passed?

Bec   Two. They were the only women.

Alex   Did you cry?

Bec   Real tears. Twenty-six times.

Beat.

I hope we have.

Alex   Bec.

Bec   No. I do. I hope we have made one. Because anything that it hurts that much to lose must be the most incredible thing to have.

Bec *is back in the pool.* **Alex** *is kneeling nearby. He plunges his arms into the water to support her.*

Alex (*he holds her hips gently or rubs her lower back*)   Is that okay?

Bec   Yes. That's good. Feels good.

Alex   Let me know what you need.

Bec   Okay.

Lights.

Scene Ten

Alex *enters the lounge on the phone. He checks that the setting is exactly right, from the lighting, to refilling* **Bec***'s water bottle. He puts on the push playlist he has created before checking that the front door is closed properly and returns to the side of the pool.*

Alex   Okay, thanks. I will. I appreciate it. Thank you.

He hangs up the call.

Bec *continues to experience stronger sensations – groaning, moaning and vocalising her experience in the pool.* **Bec** *is verbalising less and less as things are progressing. But she seems aware of what* **Alex** *is doing.*

Alex   You're doing great, Bec. Keep going. I'm so proud of you. I'm in awe of you. You make me want to be braver. I've been a shit dad before I even am one. But you, you've been the mother-load of all mothers before you even had to be. And I'm glad you're the first person the baby's gonna see because that's how it should be. You're all the parents they need and that's why – I couldn't – I didn't want to disappoint her. Him. Them. Either of you. I wasn't about to let your due date pass by like any other day. It's not, it's all I've been thinking about. *You're* all I've been thinking about. I'm sorry for leaving and I'm sorry for coming back when you didn't want either to happen. I'm sorry I wasn't by your side learning how to swaddle. I'm sorry I told you you'd ruin the carpet giving birth to our child. But I'm not sorry I'm here now. This isn't about me. I'm going to sit here and shut up and just be here if you need anything. This is all you. But if you need me, I'm here. I'm right here. Okay?

Bec *pushes. She vocalises.*

Bec   I can't!

Alex   You're doing it. You're okay. This is right. You know what to do.

Bec   I'm shit. I don't know anything. I don't know how.

Alex   You do. You can do it. You didn't need me here. Never did. You can do it, Bec.

Bec   I'm dying. I hate you. I want my mum.

Alex   You're not. It's okay.

Bec   I love you so much. I love, love, love you.

Alex   I –

The door buzzer can be heard ringing intermittently in the background the rest of the labour. **Alex** *ignores it. He immerses his arms in the pool so that he can support* **Bec***.*

Bec   I don't deserve it. I want to leave. I want to go home, Alex. I want to go home.

Alex   You are home, Bec. You're home, baby. Push.

Bec *has several contractions and on each one, she pushes.*

Bec   Oh! Yes!

Bec *delivers the baby into the water. She is the first to touch the baby, bringing her in towards her chest.* **Alex** *stands close by at the edge of the pool.*

Lights.

Transition: newborn baby crying.

Scene Eleven

Alex *is closing the front door behind the paramedics.* **Bec** *nurses the baby on the sofa. It doesn't look easy (because it isn't). There is champagne and sushi on the table.*

Alex   Thanks again, guys. Thank you. Bye. (*He turns to watch* **Bec** *and the baby silently for a little while.*) They've radioed the hospital. The midwife's about fifteen minutes away.

Bec   Really this time?

Alex   Really this time.

Bec   Are you staying?

Beat.

Until she gets here, I mean.

Alex   Right. Yeah. Till she gets here, then.

Pause.

Bec   Thank you.

Alex   Thank yourself. It was all you.

Bec (*she looks at her baby*)   I mean, for this one.

Alex   Do what I can.

Bec   Who were you speaking to, just before –

Alex (*reluctantly*)   A doula. Thanks, Google.

Bec   A hippy?

Alex   Hippy. Life saver. Same thing. Here, let me. Spicy tuna?

Bec   Okay.

Alex *feeds her while she feeds the baby.*

Bec   Will you text my mum?

Alex   Yes.

Bec   Tell her I'll call her soon. I just want a bit of this for a while first.

Alex   Yeah. I'll step out so you can –

Bec   Thanks. Dada.

Alex   That's not weird.

Bec   Really?

Alex   No, it completely is. Really strange.

Bec   I know.

Alex   I like it though.

Bec   Good. You'll be good at it.

Alex   Yeah.

Bec   Don't forget to tell her. She's a –

Alex   Wonder. My beautiful little girl.

Alex *leaves.*

Bec (*singing softly to the baby*)
   Happy birthday to you.
   Happy birthday to you.
   Happy birthday dear . . .

(*Pause. Spoken*) . . . Etta.

(*Spoken.*) Dear, dear Etta.

She kisses the baby's head.

(*Sung.*) Happy birthday to you.

Fade to black.

End of play.